Archery Basics: All About Archery

ISBN-13: 978-1479300563
ISBN-10: 147930056X

Copyright Notice

ARCHERY BASICS: ALL ABOUT ARCHERY

Steven Chramken

I dedicate this to the lucky few who've been touched by the joy, excitement and buzz of archery...

Contents

Archery:
An Introduction

Archery traces its history thousands of years back.

Over the years, stone arrowheads dating as far back as 25,000 years ago have been unearthed.

In more recent developments, even feathers attached to arrows, arrow shafts, and bows that are more than ten thousand years old have also been found.

The original purpose for which bows and arrows were made was hunting, but these items soon became deadly weapons in warfare as well.

Several different civilizations practiced archery, but it is the Egyptians who are most noted to have used it both for purposes of hunting and battle.

They are also credited for having made the world's first composite bow, although it is now believed that they got the technology from nomadic tribes who used bows on horseback.

The act of using bows of horseback, in fact, became a powerful tactic in battle.

Perhaps the most popular example of this is the way the Huns lorded it over Roman armies using archers on horseback.

They accomplished this despite the fact that Alexander the Great was able to use archers successfully in previous battles.

Other civilizations known to have used archery include the Japanese, the Chinese, the Persians, and the Indians.

A few of the famous Terracotta soldiers were themselves archers. Even the Native American tribes were known for being very proficient in archery and used it both for hunting and for battle.

Archery remained popular in eastern cultures, but it lost much of its popularity in Western Europe in the Middle Ages as a result of being viewed as a low-class tool for warfare.

However, when the English longbow was developed and it wreaked havoc on the French armies at the Battle of Agincourt, archery once again gained its lost popularity.

In Eastern cultures, it is the Chinese who are most noted for having used the crossbow since at least 2,500 years ago.

This was more forceful and ideal for shorter ranges whereas the longbow offered a huge advantage as regards the distance you could strike from.

As archery became known more and more as a powerful military tool, the art of archery also came to be practiced and celebrated in Medieval culture.

By the end of the Middle Ages, however, gun powder was invented and started being used, thus leading once again to the diminished popularity of archery on the battlefield.

Unlike before, archery was unable to regain its popularity as a military weapon owing to the continued development of more powerful and advanced weaponry even to this day.

When you talk about archery these days, it is mostly to discuss an Olympic sport that's being practiced by a considerable number of people.

There are also people these days who still use bows and arrows for hunting purposes, as they consider it a more natural and fair way of hunting as opposed to using advanced weaponry that's so easily available today.

Whatever its purpose may be, it's a fact that not many people are able to master the skill.

Archery requires steadiness, intense focus, and precision.

Whether you're stalking deer in the woods or aiming at a target on the field, there's just something alluring about the primitive nature of the sport.

Popularity of Archery

In ancient times, archery was considered as one of the best methods of fighting battles.

In fact, a number of historical epics all over the world makes mention of great archers in those days.

Archery is both a skill and an art form that involves shooting an arrow with the use of a bow to hit your target.

Warfare and hunting were the main purposes of archery in the past, but in the modern times, this art form is used mainly for recreational and sporting purposes.

There are generally two types of people who take interest in the field of archery.

The first are the archers or bowmen who actually practice the art.

The second is the toxophilite who has a deep knowledge and a profound interest in gaining more knowledge about the sport.

If you've also taken interest in archery for whatever reason, then you'd be amazed to learn that bows have been in use since the Paloelithic or Mesolithic age as evidenced by archaeological finds.

Before this era, however, it appears that bows weren't being used yet, since only arrow shafts were found to date as far back as that.

The popularity of archery even in the olden times was such that even the Chinese, Korean, and Japanese civilizations were also known to have used it extensively for warfare.

In fact, these civilizations were known to have had some of the best professional archers in their armies and these archers were a great source of pride not only to the military, but to the entire kingdom as well.

As technology advanced, however, more powerful weaponry was invented and archery lost its popularity and appeal for purposes of war.

This doesn't mean, of course, that archery is no longer popular today. It simply means that it's no longer being used for warfare.

The appeal of archery is such that people simply found different uses for it when the military lost interest.

These days, bows and arrows are popular among people who love hunting in the traditional way as well as those who have taken interest in archery as an Olympic sport.

If you're interested in learning this art form as well, then you may want to know that there are different kinds of bows used in archery.

What has become quite popular these days is the compound bow, which requires you to apply much less energy in propelling the arrow forward, thus allowing you to focus more on your target.

Arrows generally carry the same or similar designs.

It has a shaft that's shaped like an arrowhead and may be adorned on the other end with feathers known as fletchings.

The shaft of an arrow is made from several different materials such as wood, carbon fiber, fibreglass, and aluminium alloy.

You're free to choose the material that's most comfortable for you to handle.

The good thing about archery these days is that it is gaining popularity all over the world and even among women.

In fact, a lot of women have already started learning the sport and some are already competing at international levels.

Its transition from warfare to sport has indeed made archery even more appealing.

Relaxing with Archery

When you mention the word 'sport', people are likely to think about basketball, football, or tennis.

It is highly unlikely for anyone to think of archery. You may not realise it, but archery is actually a sport that's becoming more popular each year.

For many years, archery was considered a bit of a niche sport, but if people were to learn about its meditative qualities, then it would perhaps become more mainstream.

Yes, there is indeed something relaxing about the deliberate pulling back of a bowstring and then feeling the bow in your hands as you aim at your target.

And the sound of the arrow upon release brings with it a certain satisfaction that can never be fully explained to those who've never tried the sport.

Obvious evidence to the growing popularity of archery is the growing number of stores now selling archery equipment.

If you're interested in trying the sport to see if it's something you'll enjoy doing regularly, then it would be a good idea for you to go on a range and practice with their rental equipment.

You have the option of practicing with the latest and most advanced bows equipped with the latest sights.

But, if you want to know what it felt like to be an ancient archer, then you'd do well to practice with a longbow instead.

Believe it or not, archery can provide you with a unique way to unwind after a tiring day at work.

After just an hour or two on the range, you'll surely forget about whatever has made you so tired in the first place.

If competition is what you're after, then you shouldn't dismiss archery as a sport as well.

The competition in archery can be very intense and archery competitions are just as seriously fought as any football match of golf tournaments.

Competitive archery is generally known as target archery and it involves shooting a specific number of arrows at a target within a given amount of time.

The targets are set at a distance of about 30-90 metres.

The archers who participate in these competitions typically use as many technological advantages as they can along with their own skills in an effort to win the competition.

If you're not keen on competing, then you could simply join an archery club where you can fire your arrows at a target for as long as you like and at your own pace.

The beauty of archery is that you're never pressured to take part in the competitions.

Another popular form of archery you may want to try is field archery, wherein you're required to shoot in teams of five.

You may shoot with your family, friends, or colleagues.

The target in this form of archery is typically hidden in undergrowth or close to trees. As the name implies, this event takes place in the field that's usually in some woods.

Targets are positioned such that the archers have to use their judgement for calculating distance.
Shooting is often made more interesting by the pictures of animals on the targets.

Whatever form of archery you choose to engage in, you'll surely come to appreciate the relaxation you gain from the activity.

An Overview of Archery

It's no secret that archery has existed for hunting and warfare since as far back as 25,000 years ago.

Since then, archery has been an integral part of the history of many cultures.

Among the most famous archers in history are the horse archer of the Mongols and the longbow archers of the English army that wreaked havoc against the French.

Archery was, in fact, considered a key component of English society at the time and boys were compelled to practice their archery skills every Sunday.

With the invention of gun powder, however, archery slowly became obsolete on the battlefield.

The popularity of archery was revived owing to Gothic influence.

This time, however, it was no longer used for battle, but mainly for hunting, recreational, or sporting purposes.

At present, there are a number of archery clubs in many parts of the world, particularly in the United States and the United Kingdom.

The current forms of the sport are confined mainly to firing at inanimate targets, especially in places where game hunting with bows is banned.

Targets typically include animal sculptures depicting deer, rabbits, and wolves along with the more common rounded targets.

Rounded targets are typically the ones being used in competitions, particularly the Olympics and the archery world cup.

These targets have multiple colours and each of their colours corresponds to a certain point. The centre of the target typically contains a small 'x' that corresponds to ten points.

The gold-coloured area is also worth ten points whereas the red area is worth eight points, the blue worth six points, the black four points, and the white worth two points.

Any hit outside those areas is considered a miss and therefore doesn't score any point. There are, however, some competitions that use different scoring methods and point totals.

The bows currently being used belong to three general categories. The first type of bow is the recurve bow, which is the most common type and was given its name because of its flexibility as it is drawn.

This is known as the jack-of-all-trades of all bows and is often the type of bow used by beginners.

Many people also choose to continue using the recurve bow throughout their career in archery.

The second type of bow is the longbow, which is also known as the traditional bow, since it's made of wood and is usually used to shoot wooden arrows.

This bow doesn't have flexible limbs and arrows shot with it are known to glide rather than shoot through the air towards the target.

Mastering the use of the longbow is said to be the most difficult archery skill, since there are no sights, stabilisers, or gimmicks.

This may be why this is the least common of all bows.

The third type of bow is the compound bow and it is also the most expensive.

This is the most powerful type of bow, which is why it is commonly used for hunting purposes in the United States where game hunting is still allowed in certain areas.

Rather than flexible limbs, this bow uses a complex system of pulleys for drawing the arrow back and achieving a massive amount of firepower.

The arrows used with this bow are so powerful that there's a need to use special targets in competitions. Archery is indeed a sport that's rich in history and popularity.

Archery Equipment

Archery is indeed an amazing sport. If you're interested in learning and mastering archery skills, then you'd do well to learn more about the basic equipment needed.

1. The main archery equipment is, of course, the bow. There are different types of bow and you'll have to learn how each of them works in order to determine which type of bow is the best for you.

   When you visit an archery shop, you're likely to find bamboo-backed longbows, youth longbows, custom longbows, medieval longbows, and many other types of bow. You'd do well to try handling each type of bow to see how it feels in your hands and to determine which one feels most comfortable.

2. The bowstring is another important element, as it is what gives the bow its curved appearance. Most of the existing bowstrings are made from synthetic fibre materials, animal materials, and plant fibres. The centre of a bowstring is typically a thread that's used to provide support to the arrow.

3. Of course, you can't practice archery without an arrow. Just are different types of bow, there are also several different types of arrow currently being sold.

   These include youth arrows, cedar hunting arrows, lacquered cedar arrows, cedar classic arrows, and gold tip carbon arrows, among other choices. Your choice of arrows will depend on the type of bow you use and the features you want your arrows to have.

4. Another important element is that shaft, which is the tip of the arrow. Traditional arrow shafts are typically made from wood, particularly cedar.

   These days, however, there are many archers who use arrow shafts made from carbon, aluminium, fibreglass, and composite materials.

   Wooden arrow shafts are commonly used by beginners owing to the lightness of the materials. Bow hunters and archery competitors often prefer using aluminium arrow shafts.

You may want to note that carbon arrow shafts are best able to maintain velocity because they are highly wind resistant.

5. The point is also an essential component in archery. It is found on the arrowhead and often made from various materials such as metal and other hard materials.

6. Fletch is what you'd usually find on the other end of the arrow. Most of these things are made from plastic or feathers. The purpose of the fletch is to keep your arrow moving straight towards your target.

7. Other than the right equipment, you should also wear the appropriate clothing for archery. This helps you ensure that you're comfortable as you shoot. You're going to need gear such as a chest guard, arm guards, slings, and the tab.

These are just some of the most basic things you need to have as you start learning the sport of archery.

You may want to rent equipment to start with until you're sure that archery is something you'll definitely enjoy doing for a long time.

You may then start buying only the most essential pieces of equipment and then simply adding other items as your skill improve and especially if you decide to train for becoming a competitive archer.

Tips for Beginners

Archery can be among the best hobbies to pursue. It can teach you a lot about patience and learning to focus.

The good news is that this isn't a very expensive sport to start learning. But, of course, you'll have to invest a little more in the sport as your skills grow and if you decide to progress to the professional levels.

As a beginner, you're likely to experience a bit of frustration in learning the fundamentals of the sport. You're likely to miss on your first few shots or even fail to launch the arrow properly. To ease your frustration, bear in mind that you're not really expected to be an excellent marksman at the outset.

What you need to do is take a number of things into consideration as you start learning the art of archery.

1. Choose Your Equipment

Choosing your bow and arrows carefully helps you ensure that you can maximise your archery skills.

It may be a good idea to start with a lightweight bow you can comfortably pull. You may move on to heavier bows as your skills improve. You should also remember to take proper care of your equipment and keep it in good condition.

2. Be Consistent

Anchor points are the place where you need to consistently pull the bowstring back to. Most beginners use the point at which the index finger of their drawing hand reaches just below their chin as the anchor point.

The bowstring should barely touch the tip of your nose in this case. You may also try other anchor points until you find the most comfortable and then you should use this anchor point consistently.

3. Grip the Bow Properly

Many beginners think they should grip the bow very tightly, but you need to realise this will only give you a less accurate throw.

That's because an extremely tight grip will likely make your bow twist and rotate as you take the shot.

You should hold the bow loosely instead in order to make a straight shot.

4. Follow Through

Always remember to follow through with your shot. To follow through, you need to keep your bow arm up and your eyes focused on the target. Beginners typically make the mistake of lowering their bow too soon, which gives the arrow a downward force. This mistake can cost you several shots that would have scored big so you need to avoid it at all times.

5. Concentrate

Needless to say, concentration is crucial in archery. Aim at your target for about ten seconds before releasing the arrow and be sure to focus your whole attention on your target.

6. Relax

Avoid being tense as you shoot. Control your breathing, take a few deep breaths, and be sure to release the last deep breath very slowly as you release the bowstring. Being relaxed allows you to concentrate more and therefore helps increase the accuracy of your shots.

7. Practice

As always, practice makes perfect in archery. As mentioned above, you're not expected to make perfect shots on your first try. As you continue practicing, though, you should be able to increase your accuracy and shooting skills.

More importantly, you should be patient as you learn the fundamentals of archery. Don't be too hard on yourself when you don't get it right the first time. Just enjoy the activity and relax.

Determining Arrow Length

One of the things you'll have to ensure when you start learning archery is that the arrows you use are of the right length.

There are, of course, a few things you need to consider when trying to find the right arrow length.

In this section, you'll learn some tips on finding the right arrow length to be used with a compound bow, which is currently the most widely-used type of bow.

Just like in many other sports, speed is a very important element in archery. This is why arrow manufacturers are fiercely competing with each other in producing the fastest arrows.

Take note that an arrow's speed is typically dictated by two things: its weight and its length.

The general rule is that the lighter an arrow is, the faster it can fly.

Remember, though, that an arrow that's too light can damage your bow, while an arrow that's too heavy could lose trajectory. You therefore have to choose the arrow's weight very carefully.

In the same way, you'll have to carefully choose your arrow's length.

The general rule is that the longer an arrow is, the heavier it is likely to be.

It therefore makes sense that everyone would want to go for short lightweight arrows.

Take note, however, that arrows that are too short may cause injuries if it gets lodged behind the rest at full draw. It could snap and shatter on release, thus injuring your hand and arm.

An arrow that's too short could also have broadhead clearance issues. The general rule is that if the broadhead cuts your fingers when you shoot, then the arrow is too short. Try not to discover that the hard way.

One of the most effective ways to determine that right arrow length is for you to use the draw-and-measure method.

You should get the help of someone else to accomplish this task. Let the other person stand safely to the side as you draw your bow to full draw with an arrow shaft in place.

Have the other person mark the shaft just in front of the arrow shelf.

This should give your broadhead enough clearance.

Now, you need to measure the area of the arrow shaft from the mark to the nock. The resulting measurement will then be the best arrow length for you.

Where the weight of your arrow is concerned, the industry standard sets a weight minimum of 5 grains per pound of bow.

This means that if your bow weighs 50 pounds, then your arrow should weight 250 grains. This includes the tip weight and is set for purposes of bow health and your own safety.

In the United States, there are different arrow weight regulations in different states and it is your responsibility to learn and adhere to your state's regulations.

Once you've determined the right arrow length, you may start finding the best arrow weight for you. And then you should be ready to start shopping for your very own set of arrows.

Measuring Draw Length

Just as it is important for you to determine the right length for your arrows, it is also important to determine the correct draw length needed for you to be able to effectively shoot a compound bow.

In most cases, the right draw length is the same as the length of arrow you use, but it can vary from one person to the next.

Take note as well that there are a number of more accurate ways to measure the right draw length than simply relying on the length of your arrows.

One of the first things you should bear in mind is that it's important for you to feel comfortable with the entire setup of your archery equipment.

Your comfort level may give you a general idea of what draw length you should be using, but you may still have to make some slight adjustments.

The good thing is that it's easy enough to alter the draw length on most compound bows.

If you plan to buy a previously used compound bow, then you'll most likely have to do this.

Here are some of the most effective ways to measure the correct draw length:

1. Perhaps the easiest way to measure draw length is to take your own height and then divide it by 2.5. The result you come up with is the approximate draw length that you need.

   Take note, though, that this is considered as the least accurate method of measurement for the simple reason that it automatically assumes that your arm span is the same as your own height.

   Everyone is physically built differently, so this may not really be true for some people.

2. Another method of measuring draw length is to hold your fist out in front of you and then measuring the distance from the front of your fist to your mouth. The result you come up with is likely the right draw length for you because this is the way a bow will be held.

The downside of this method is that it automatically assumes that you're in the proper stance. This may not really be true of beginners, which means it may not really be very accurate.

3. The third method of measuring draw length is based on the first and is considered as a much more accurate method. The measurement is taken by holding your arms out at shoulders length with your fingers pointing outwards.

    Ask someone else to measure the distance between the tips of your two middle fingers. Just like in the first method, you should divide the measurement by 2.5 and the result should be your draw length.

    Since this method allows for differences in arm span, it is a more preferable method.

It helps for you to understand all three methods of measuring draw length because they all have their own set of advantages and disadvantages.

If you're still in doubt and you're not very confident about taking the measurements by yourself, then you'd best visit an archery store and get yourself measured there.

Try to avoid changing your draw length too often, since a consistent contact point allows you to achieve consistency in your shots as well.

Preparing for Archery Training

The art of marksmanship using bows and arrows has been popular for thousands of years. Since it started being practiced, people have loved learning about archers and what they do.

An archer is generally defined as someone who is skilled with a bow and arrow, and has developed the ability to shoot targets on sight.

The act of shooting arrows towards targets may look easy, but it's not. One requires a considerable amount of practice in order to ensure correct stance, positioning, and shooting technique as well as to master the art.

For a beginner, it can be very difficult to practice different techniques and figure out which are the most effective ones.

You'll have to adapt to your surroundings before you even take your first shot. This is the reason why an adequate amount of training is very important.

Unless you learn and master the basic techniques for shooting an arrow, you'll never be able to excel in the sport of archery.

Among other important things, you'll have to learn how to properly hold the bow and how you should draw the arrow.

You'll have to sort through a number of intricacies to make sure you properly learn the basics of shooting an arrow.

If you're serious about starting a career in archery, then you'd do well to join a club where professionals could teach you how to become an excellent marksman.

More importantly, you'll have to gain an understanding of the traits of a good archer.

As mentioned above, the first thing you need to practice in your efforts to become an excellent archer is to hold the bow properly. Your stance, positioning, and the manner with which you take a shot is very important.

Unless you're able to accomplish this first step, you'll never be able to take a good shot, no matter how good your archery equipment is.

It's a good idea for you to take a demo class before signing up for archery lessons so you can determine if the instructor has the ability to convey his messages clearly and effectively instruct you on how to properly hold a bow and take aim.

This is because it's important for you to understand the aiming process very well.

One of the most common beliefs people have is that you need to take aim with one of your eyes closed. As you keep practicing, though, you'll realise that there are techniques for aiming and shooting with both eyes open.

What you need to do to achieve this purpose is establish a good balance between your dominant eye and your non-dominant eye. Of course, you should also make sure your aim is accurate enough.

In most cases, the best way to do that is to trust your instincts. In fact, your sixth sense is sometimes the most important element you need to consider in order to become really good in archery.

As soon as you get the feeling that it's the right time to shoot, then you should immediately release the arrow. This increases your chances for a successful shot.

These are just of the useful tips you can use when you're just starting out as an archer.

What's important is for you to relax and just enjoy the sport. Archery training may be difficult, but it doesn't have to take the fun out of the sport.

Practice Tips

Archery can be defined simply as a sport that involves shooting with a bow and arrow.

Although the fundamentals of getting off a shot aren't really that tough, the act of trying to master the sport and achieve proficiency in it can be very challenging.

As a beginner, you'd do well to concentrate on first mastering the basics of shooting with a bow and arrow.

This may not be a sport for everyone, but those who engage in archery definitely find it to be a lot of fun and something you'll surely want to do better in.

Following are a number of archery practice tips that can help you master the basic archery techniques and be your first step towards increased accuracy, more enjoyment, and a better appreciation of the sport.

Perhaps the most important thing you need to ensure as a beginner in archery is that you use the proper technique.

For this you need proper posture and a good sense of balance. You need to position your feet comfortably apart to achieve balance.

Furthermore, you should keep your arm straight as you draw the bowstring and you should bring your draw hand carefully back to touch your face.

You should also keep yourself relaxed as you take aim and release the string to propel the arrow towards your target.

Once you learn this basic motion and develop your skills in it, your confidence will surely grow and you'll be in a better position to perfect the move.

A lot of beginners make the mistake of gripping the bow too tightly. Take note that this can cause the bow to twist and turn, thus throwing off your shot.

Always remember to keep your grip firm yet relaxed. As for the bowstring, the traditional three-finger grip should suffice for beginners.

This grip requires you to hold your index finger above the nock and then your ring and middle fingers below the nock.

Make sure there's enough space between your index and middle finger to avoid pinching the nock. You should also make sure there's equal pressure applied by each of your three fingers to the string.

As you draw the bowstring back, be sure to pause at your anchor point before releasing the string. Determining a consistent anchor point is one of the keys to developing accuracy in your shots.

This is the exact point where your draw hand rests in front of your face before the string is released. A good way of determining your anchor point is to draw the string to the point where your index finger will barely touch the side of your chin.

If this gives you a good shot, then you should strive to anchor all of your shots from that point.

Remember that what you're aiming for is consistency. You should also follow through on every shot you take. You may want to keep your bow up until the arrow actually hits the target.

Bear all these tips in mind as you start learning how to shoot properly with a bow and arrow.

You should be comfortable enough with the sport in no time at all.

Techniques

As a beginner in the sport of archery, it's very important for you to learn the different methods by which you can shoot an arrow with a bow.

An archer is typically defined according to his accuracy and precision.

His skill is also measured based on the flexibility with which he is able to dispatch his arrows.

There have been several different archery techniques discovered and practiced over the years and the latest technological advancements have also introduced a wide variety of methods by which an archer can shoot his arrows.

What's most important to an archer is the ability to hit accurate shots within a small period of time.

There are many archers who need to get into a certain position in order to shoot accurately. For example, you may have to crouch or rest your elbow on something in order for you to shoot properly.

Other than the shooting position, though, there are now accessories you can use to help improve your accuracy as well.

The most basic of these accessories are the arm guard and the finger tab, which can greatly increase your chances for getting off a successful shot with your bow and arrow.

Another effective way of ensuring an accurate shot is to make sure your body is properly aligned with your bow such that your eye can pinpoint the exact area you'll be shooting at when you take aim.

Remember that archery doesn't simply involve pulling back the bowstring and then letting go in hopes that the arrow will automatically hit its target.

There are several different things you need to take into consideration as you shoot.

For one thing, your back muscles need to be held just tight enough to ensure the right amount of tension that'll reduce the recoil reaction of shooting, but you should also make sure you're relaxed enough not to lose focus on your target.

Your draw hand in particular needs to be sufficiently relaxed when you release the string. When there's too much tension in your draw hand, the arrow is bound to be thrown off-balance.

It's also important for you to learn the proper positioning of your bow arm. You need to keep this arm up and steady when you shoot to make sure your arrow doesn't go anywhere but towards the target.

It's crucial for an archer to be able to keep his movements steady and position himself such that he doesn't make any sudden movements.

Naturally, skilled professionals are able to take much quicker shots than amateurs, simply because they've learned how to steady themselves within split-seconds and then draw and release within the blink of an eye.

Practice plays a very important role in developing this ability. The more you practice basic positioning, the quicker you'll be able to take aim and make your shot.

These are just some of the tips and techniques you can make use of when you start learning the sport of archery.

Perhaps the most important thing to bear in mind is for you to simply relax, have fun, and enjoy the sport.

Improving Your Accuracy

Consistency is the key to becoming a great archer. Regardless of what your current skill level is, you won't be able to reach your true potential for accuracy in archery unless you develop consistency in your shots.

If you're like most beginners, then you're likely wondering how you can develop consistency. The answer is actually quite simple: You just have to make use of anchor points.

What are anchor points in the first place?

An anchor point is simply defined as the exact place where you reach full draw and pause before releasing the bowstring to propel the arrow towards the target.

If, for example, the knuckle of your index finger touches the underside of your earlobe at full draw, this is your anchor point. In order to achieve consistency in your shots, you'll have to shoot from this point every single time.

If this particular anchor point doesn't give you a very good shot, then you just have to make some slight adjustments.

Now the next question that'll probably come to mind is if anchor points are indeed necessary.

Well, the value of anchor points lies in the fact that it's very rare for a beginner in archery to draw the bowstring into the exact same position every time he draws.

This results in one shot being dead on and the next one too far away from the target. Again, you need to bear in mind that consistency is the key to improving your accuracy in the sport of archery.

The simple technique of using anchor points works so well that it may be safe to say it is indeed necessary if you truly want to develop accuracy in your shots because it allows you to make sure that you're shooting from the exact same spot all the time.

The most common anchor points are the knuckle of your index finger touching the underside of your earlobe, the bowstring touching the tip of your nose, the knuckle of your index finger behind your jaw bone, and the kisser button touching the corner of your mouth.

Your choice of anchor point will depend on factors such as the type of bow you use, your draw length, the hardware on your bow, and the type of release you use.

An anchor point could be practically anything as long as it doesn't put you or anyone else in danger.
More importantly, it should be something you can easily find every single time you take a shot.

One thing that's commonly advised to beginners in archery is to incorporate two to three anchor points into their shooting routine.

This helps you ensure that you'll be drawing to the same general area, if not the exact same point, every time you take aim.

You'd do well to heed this advice if you seriously want to ramp up your accuracy in the sport of archery. Who knows, this could very well be the start of a long and successful career in one of the world's oldest sports.

When to Replace
Your Strings

Regardless of whether you choose to use a recurve, compound, or crossbow, the bowstring will always be one of their most important components.

The bowstring can have a lot of functions, but its main function is to draw back the bow's limbs, thus making it possible for you to shoot the arrow towards your target.

You need to bear in mind that the bowstring is being constantly placed under a considerable amount of pressure whether you're drawing it or it's just sitting there unused.

It goes without saying, therefore, that you'll have to replace your bowstring after some time. But, how exactly do you know when the bowstring needs replacing?

Here are the signs you need to watch for so you'll know it's the right time to change your string:

1. Fraying

This doesn't mean you should immediately replace your string the moment you see a few minor frayed strands in some parts of the string.

Such minor fraying is actually normal and can easily be fixed by rubbing bow wax onto the string.

However, if your bowstring starts to look as if a bird has attempted to build its nest there, then it is definitely time for you to look for a replacement.

2. Breakage

It's practically obvious why you need to replace your bowstring once breakage occurs. To make it clear, though, if one or two strands of the string are broken, but the rest are still pretty much in good condition, then you may still be able to shoot like you always do. However, you should always keep an eye out for further breakage at this point. It's advisable to use your best judgement in this case.

3. Strand Separation

This tends to occur as the bowstring ages, if it isn't waxed regularly or maintained properly, or if the bow is made to sit for extended periods without being used.

When this happens, the strands of the bowstring will look separated and loose.

They could also become rotted and brittle, which can cause some major issues, since the string could snap the next time you use it, thus causing damage to your bow or injury to you.

These are the three most common signs you need to look out for in order to determine whether your bowstring needs to be replaced.

Now, here's an additional word of caution: If you ever dry fire your bow, which is to say you fired the bow without loading an arrow, then you'll most probably need to replace the string afterwards.

The best thing to do in this case is to have an authorized bow technician check your string and advise you as to whether it does indeed need replacing or not.

As long as you take good care of your bowstring and maintain its integrity and durability using bow wax, then it should serve you for a long time.

Furthermore, you should store your bow properly and your bowstring will surely be able to provide you with more than a hundred shots.

Fitness for Archery

Archery seems like such a relaxed sport that you just may think it's not important to engage in a fitness routine to excel in this sport. In most cases, archery isn't considered as a physically demanding sport.

But, just like many other physical endeavours, your performance can definitely be improved if you have proper physical conditioning.

Therefore, a few exercises that include a moderate strength training routine should be considered if you're serious about taking your archery skills to a higher level and if you want to reach your full potential in the sport.

Other than steady nerves and a good eye, you'll be sure to benefit from having stronger shoulder back, and arm muscles.

This is what makes it a good idea to add the right strength training program to your fitness routine for archery. As you get stronger, you should be able to increase your draw.

Consequently, this will give your arrow a much better flight trajectory.

Increased strength will also allow you to maintain good balance and keeps your aim steady, thus providing you with better archery results.

If you also choose to go bow hunting, then you'll definitely benefit from being able to hike longer distances and carry large game easily.

Strength training will also help reduce the risk for joint and tendon injury, which often develops due to repeated shooting with a bow and arrow.

A good fitness program for archery doesn't take much time to provide you with good conditioning and strength gains.

For upper body conditioning, it's best to perform exercises that work your shoulder muscles, upper back muscles, and chest muscles. To be specific, your shoulder muscles can benefit from overhead presses and lateral raises.

Your back muscles may be strengthened with seated rows, chin-ups, and lat put-downs. You may then work your chest muscles with bench presses, chest flyes, and push-ups.

All of these exercises can be performed with either free weights or weight machines. The good thing is that most gyms offer a wide array of options for you to work these muscle groups.

One thing you should always bear in mind when you do strength training is the importance of always using proper form as well as slow and controlled movements.

Remember as well to always work through a full range of motion when you exercise.

It's advisable for you to with high repetitions for just a set or two at least twice each week. And while it's important to focus on your shoulders, back, and chest, you also shouldn't forget to work your legs.

You should therefore include some squats, leg presses, and lunges in your exercise routine. Stronger legs will surely help with stabilization as you draw, aim, and shoot.

Remember that you're not required to spend too much time on strength training, but it's definitely advisable to include it in your archery training routine.

You'll soon find that the task of holding the bow, drawing the string, and holding it steady as you aim and shoot is so much easier with increased strength.

And now you can concentrate more on aiming and ensuring accuracy with every shot.

Preparing for Competition

Among the ultimate goals of many archers is to reach a skill level that'll allow them to compete in archery tournaments, whether big or small.

They want to build a reputation in their chosen sport. They want other archers and archery enthusiasts to recognize their name. It is their aim to earn that trophy and belong to the best players in their field.

The achievement of finally reaching this goal can indeed be so fulfilling along with proving to yourself that you can be the best and your years of hard work does pay off.

If this also your ultimate goal and you want to do well in this sport, then you'd surely want to know how you can get yourself ready for competition.

You need to know what you should do in order to reach what you're aiming for, which is to be known in this sport.

Whatever competition you plan to join, preparation is indeed extremely important. In the case of archery, the required preparation includes proper training and constant practice.

Training doesn't just refer to getting proper instructions in archery techniques. It also includes fitness training to properly condition and strengthen your body.

You need to be able to sustain proper posture throughout the archery tournament you decide to join, which is why strength and conditioning training is necessary.

You'll have to develop muscle endurance as well because getting tired easily can affect your performance towards the end of the competition, just when you're getting near your goal of winning top prize.

You have to be able to maintain your focus, your consistency, and your accuracy, which is why you need to be strong and fit.

Other than that, you should also make sure you practice in the right location. What does this mean?

It means you need to do your homework and find out what the conditions are in the place where the competition is to be held. What is the climate in the area?

Is it too warm, too cold, or too windy? Once you find out the conditions in the competition venue, you need to find a place near your area with similar conditions and then spend your practice sessions there.

This helps you make the necessary adjustments to your shooting. It will also let you know if you need to make some adjustments to your physical fitness training routine.

For example, if the venue of competition is in a high-altitude area, then you may have to do some aerobic exercises to increase your endurance in such areas.

Another thing you need to make sure of is that every piece of your archery equipment is properly maintained and always kept in the best condition possible.

It would also be a good idea to have a spare set of equipment on hand just in case your primary equipment gets damaged in any way.

It can be very frustrating to have to bow out of competition simply because your equipment got damaged and you don't have a replacement at the ready.

So, now that you know what you need to do to prepare for an archery competition, you should be ready to start competing and working towards the fulfilment of your goal.

Good luck!

15169601R00057

Printed in Great Britain
by Amazon.co.uk, Ltd.,
Marston Gate.